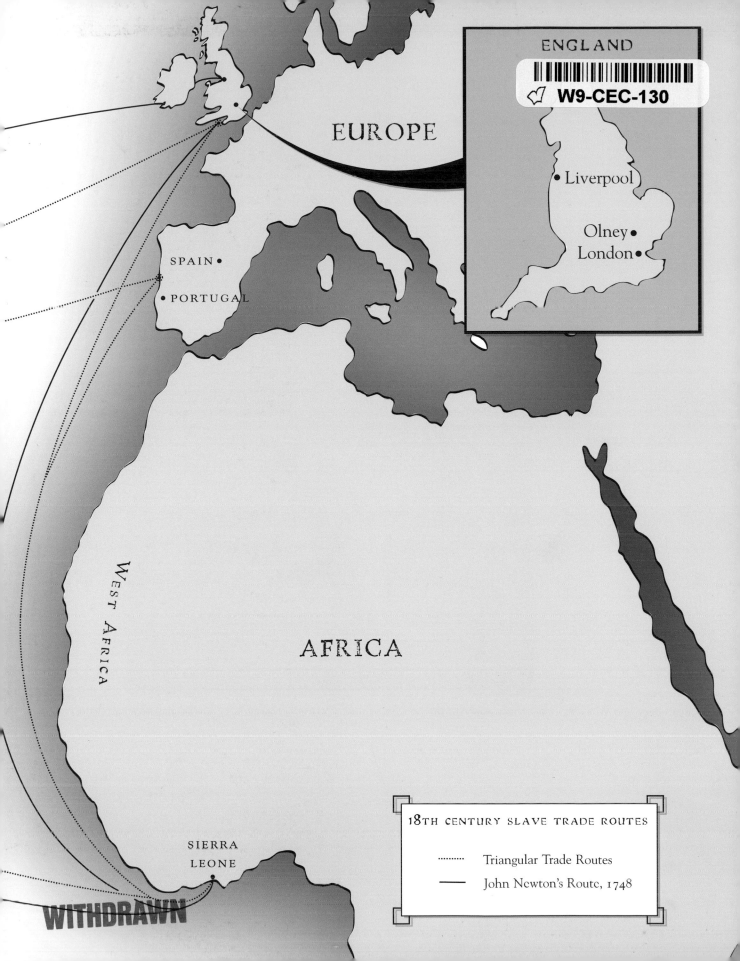

EUROPE

Liverpool

Olney
London

SPAIN •

• PORTUGAL

WEST AFRICA

AFRICA

SIERRA
LEONE

18TH CENTURY SLAVE TRADE ROUTES

.......... Triangular Trade Routes

——— John Newton's Route, 1748

For my daughter, Devon Marie Smiley, who never ceases to amaze – L.G.

To the villagers of Eden Mills, for their kindness and grace – J.W.

# Out of Slavery

## The Journey to Amazing Grace

Linda Granfield

Illustrated by Janet Wilson

Tundra Books

Originally published as *Amazing Grace: The Story of the Hymn*, 1997

The author and illustrator express their gratitude to the Tundra crew, especially Kathy Lowinger, who captained this craft. Thanks to Michael Seary, the Toronto Reference Library; the Maritime Museum of the Atlantic; Catherine McLean, Toronto Brigantine; Rick Moss, Museum of Black History; Rector Nigel Pond, Olney, England; Barb de Kat; Trish Hill; and Llewellyn, Marguerite, Jamaal, and Gary. Cal Smiley and Chris Wilson deserve special mention as admirable first mates. And finally, thanks to the many historians, biographers, and artists who, through the centuries, passionately chronicled the struggles of the world's enslaved peoples.

Published in Canada by Tundra Books,
75 Sherbourne Street, Toronto, Ontario M5A 2P9

Published in the United States by Tundra Books of Northern New York,
P.O. Box 1030, Plattsburgh, New York 12901

Library of Congress Control Number: 96-61146

**Library of Archives Canada Cataloguing in Publication**
Granfield, Linda
Out of slavery : the journey to Amazing grace / Linda Granfield ; illustrated
by Janet Wilson.
Previously published under title: Amazing grace.
ISBN 978-0-88776-915-3
1. Newton, John, 1725-1807–Juvenile literature. 2. Amazing grace (Hymn)–
Juvenile literature. 3. Clergy–England–Biography–Juvenile literature. 4. Hymn
writers–England–Biography–Juvenile literature. 5. Slave traders–England–
Biography–Juvenile literature. I. Wilson, Janet, 1952- II. Granfield, Linda.
Amazing grace. III. Title.
BX5199.N55G72 2009                 j264'.23092                 C2008-905752-X
We acknowledge the financial support of the Government of Canada through the Book Publishing Industry Development Program (BPIDP) and that of the Government of Ontario through the Ontario Media Development Corporation's Ontario Book Initiative. We further acknowledge the support of the Canada Council for the Arts and the Ontario Arts Council for our publishing program.

ONTARIO ARTS COUNCIL
CONSEIL DES ARTS DE L'ONTARIO

Printed and bound in Canada

1  2  3  4  5  6          14  13  12  11  10  09

# Out of Slavery

In the oppressive night-blackness, the horizon melted into the sea as the *African* moved towards the West Indies. Seamen, soaked with spray, struggled on deck and never noticed the beauty of the vicious, glitter-tipped waves that tossed the vessel. Like a living creature, the ship responded noisily. The *African*'s oak timbers groaned as the dark waters heaved across the deck and deeply sighed when the waves' weight crashed back into the sea. The masts strained and moaned in the relentless winds.

Below deck, the cargo shifted with each wrenching wave and echoed the timbers' moans. Metal clanked as the *African* pitched again. In the unlit bowels of the vessel, a seaman saw little and choked as he tried to breathe the putrid, stifling air. Huge waves licked and pitched the ship again. The cargo, and the sailor's stomach, lurched, and he hurried out. Better to risk being swept away, rather than stay where it wasn't fit for man or beast. The cargo be damned!

Damnation was also on the mind of Captain John Newton as he tracked the *African*'s progress on the charts in his quarters. The vessel had left Liverpool, England, in July 1752, bound for West Africa and farther. The voyage would take more than a year. Newton had weathered fiercer storms and with worse crews, but he'd also spent many hours each day praying for guidance. With the Lord's help, Newton would successfully deliver his cargo of 207 African men, women, and children to be sold in the marketplaces of the West Indies. As the vessel was lashed again by the heaving waves, the slave trader wondered how much of the cargo would survive the trip.

The sea carried John Newton on its back for nearly thirty years. Born in London in 1725, he was the son of a sea captain and a devout mother, who taught her only child at home. By the time he was four, Newton could read, and he memorized biblical quotations, hymns, and poems. At six, he began to learn Latin, the language he would need if he were to become a minister, as his mother wished.

In 1737, eleven-year-old John was taken by his father to sea for the first time. Many voyages would follow. Newton spent his teen years in conflict, torn between his early religious education and the challenges of life at sea. He wrote, "I had little concern about religion and easily received very ill impressions."

A seaman's life was one of hardship. Voyages lasted for years, and poor working conditions meant a man could be maimed for life or die of disease, malnourishment, or even murder while en route. Since men didn't always readily volunteer for the navy or business sailing, the government or private businessmen had to offer incentives. Notices described the ships' destinations as if they were pleasure resorts, offering plenty of rum, sugar, and money if a man signed on, for example, for a voyage to Jamaica.

When the inviting notices failed to bring in men, the last resort was the press-gang. A group of seamen visited taverns or poorer sections of coastal towns, chose a "victim," and kidnapped him, sometimes with a great deal of force. Thousands of men became seamen in this way. Others taken onboard included criminals released from prisons and poor laborers, who sold themselves to the merchants and sent their low wages home to famished relatives.

Inadequate clothing, maggot-ridden food, and harsh justice onboard ships left few seamen in a generous frame of mind when human cargo was delivered into their care.

Slavery had existed long before John Newton was born. In ancient times, Egyptian, Greek, Roman, and Chinese armies gathered the people they conquered and enslaved them. During Newton's lifetime, nearly 5,000 slaving voyages left from Liverpool alone. Meanwhile, other European countries like Spain and Portugal sent slave ships, or slavers, to Africa. It is impossible to know exactly how many millions of Africans were enslaved. Records were poorly kept, sometimes on purpose. Many Africans perished en route to the slave ships. Hundreds more died onboard.

When John Newton became involved in the slave business, he was not breaking any laws. Legitimate merchants owned the slavers, laden with goods like kettles, weapons, and kegs of rum to exchange for captives. Commerce fueled the entire operation. The Americas supplied cotton, sugar, and coffee to be exported to Europe, and cheap human labor was needed to gather the goods. As production boomed, more workers were needed, and Europe turned to Africa to meet the growing demand for laborers.

Vessels sailed to West Africa and anchored offshore, and the captain watched for smoke signals on the beach – the sign that the resident slave dealers had captives for sale. Settlements along the coast of Sierra Leone were Newton's particular destinations.

The dealers kept up with Europe's demand for slaves by kidnapping Africans or by manipulating the local political leaders. Africans were captured during skirmishes; enemies sold one another to the dealers. Yoked together with crude wooden devices, the captives from the inlands of Africa were marched or taken by boat to the coast.

A longboat was sent to shore by the captain and the bargaining began. The negotiations could be dangerous as arguments broke out, for no one wanted to be cheated. In his *Journal of a Slave Trader*, Newton wrote about the business of buying slaves. He complained that the purchase was going too slowly. He wanted people who were "sizeable" and wrote that many brought to him were under four feet tall. In the *Journal*, it becomes obvious that Newton didn't want to be taken for a fool when dealers brought him captives with rotten teeth, sagging bosoms, or crippling malformations. He refused those who were "lame, old or blind." Each slave had to be well-formed and extremely healthy in order to have a chance of surviving the voyage, and then they had to be able to work and breed for the new masters.

Prices were debated and finally agreed upon. The purchased slaves lost their freedom and their names. They were assigned numbers, chained to prevent escape, and often branded. They were shaved to prevent the spread of lice and taken into the hold of the slaver, again, to prevent escape. (Many captured Africans chose to drown off the coast of their homeland, rather than be taken by the strangers – and such deaths meant lost money.) If a family had been taken to the shore, it was separated onboard: men in one section, women and children in another. The languages of many African tribes mingled with the shouted commands up on deck as the slaver moved further along the West African coast and added to its cargo.

Some slave traders were called "tight packers" because they bought until the ship was overflowing. Such traders knew a large percentage of the slaves would die of "the flux" (dysentery) or other diseases while at sea. They wanted to arrive with a profitable number, regardless. Others, like Newton, were "loose packers," who hoped to arrive in Antigua with healthier slaves who had benefited from what the captain considered better accommodations.

For eight weeks or longer, the slaves endured the Middle Passage, the portion of the slave-trade triangle from Africa to the Americas and the Caribbean. While the seamen enjoyed fresh air performing their duties on deck, the hundreds of humans below suffered from stifling heat and limited movement. Below deck, there were approximately one and a half meters (five feet), floor-to-ceiling, for people to stand up. Some captains divided the space in half with a platform in order to stuff as many slaves as possible in the same area. This platform allowed each person fewer than seventy-six centimeters (thirty inches) in which to crouch.

Movement was further restricted by chains. The slaves were chained to each other; the right foot and hand of one shackled to the left foot and hand of another. If one slave died, he remained bound to the living until one of the crew came to help. Epidemics of the flux and smallpox killed many and the ship's surgeon could do little. The dead were tossed overboard without ceremony. According to Newton's *Journal*, after a death the lower deck was "smoked with tar, tobacco and brimstone [sulphur] for two hours, [and] afterwards washed with vinegar" in order to discourage the spread of contagion. The smell of such cleansers blended with the odors of overflowing slop buckets, sweat, and near-death.

Rats shared the space with the cargo, which included thousands of pounds of rice to feed the Africans. Records show that John Newton's captives had bread for breakfast and one hot meal each day. (In fact, Newton complained about the lack of money for two hot meals.) Periodically, the slaves were taken into the salty air on the upper deck. There, they were chained to the deck (to prevent them from jumping overboard) and splashed with cold water in an attempt to keep them healthy.

Babies were born. Some were accepted as bonus slaves, but more often, infants were seen as more trouble than they were worth and were tossed overboard. Segregated from any who could protect them, the women were victimized by the seamen. It's no wonder that the slaves themselves, despite the many languages they spoke, understood each other's desire for freedom and conspired to overthrow their captors and take the vessel back home. Newton, like many other captains, discovered such a plan and searched the slaves' quarters. He found knives and stones waiting to be clasped by shackled hands and applied to the chests and heads of the seamen. Since such an insurrection would result in the possible loss of everyone onboard, and the certain loss of money, even less monstrous captains, like Newton, had to punish the perpetrators: "Put the boys in irons and slightly in the thumbscrew to urge them to a full confession." The men identified were put into heavy, painful metal collars.

Newton's actions, related in his numerous publications, are astounding. During his teen years, he himself had been enslaved on a lime plantation in Sierra Leone by an unscrupulous slave dealer. Clothed in rags, the youth slept in the rain and struggled to survive, without a word of kindness, without human touch. For fifteen months he endured, befriended by the Africans he worked amongst, and then rejoiced when delivered into freedom by a sea captain.

Newton knew from his own experience what it was to be enslaved. Yet, he took part in the sale of humans. While he referred to them as "men" and "women," not cargo, he nevertheless carried them off to Antigua to be distributed like so much corn, sold to the highest bidder. It is easy for modern readers to say he should have known better; to his contemporaries, and to himself, John Newton was simply taking care of British business.

Despite primitive navigational instruments and human miscalculations, slavers like the *African* managed to deliver their cargoes to the New World. Just offshore, the slaves were washed and freshly shaved. Some were rubbed with oil to enhance the darkness of their skin (and camouflage any signs of illness).

After the sale of the slaves, the captain turned his attention to filling the vessel with supplies and marketable goods. (Newton's cargo once included "74 hogsheads [of rum], 4 tierces [old measure] of sugar and 23 bags of cotton.") With her crew replenished, the slaver set sail and arrived about seven weeks later in England. The captain received his salary and a share in the profits. The ship's surgeon received head money for each slave who survived the journey to the New World. The triangular voyage was complete.

The period of John Newton's lifetime (1725-1807) was one of the most explosive in the world's history. "Wretchedness" was a constant theme in the writing of the time. The word *revolution* was often heard. There was the Industrial Revolution: Newly invented machinery and the factory system moved people from the countryside into polluted cities incapable of handling the masses. Enslaved by the prosperous merchants, children aged eight and younger worked in textile mills for thirteen hours a day, at least six days a week. As a result, more than one generation of children grew up with no education. The gap between the wealthy and the poor widened. Destitution and death were written about and portrayed in art.

In North America, New France had fallen to the British. And during the American Revolution, the colonies gained their independence from Britain. Thousands of families were torn apart as soldiers were recruited and never seen again. The British government, under the chronically ill King George III, had a difficult time convincing people that everything was secure; there were seven different prime ministers in a ten-year period.

In nearby France, another violent revolution was brewing. There, as in England, the people's misery grew. Speakers all around the world began to emotionally proclaim about freedom and human rights. The crowds listening to them grew larger.

Meanwhile, the slave ships continued to transport the profitable human cargoes.

Throughout his life at sea, John Newton alternately embraced and abandoned religion. He had a reputation for swearing, and he admitted to making a nuisance of himself onboard, undermining his captain any way he could, such as inventing clever songs that ridiculed him. The other seamen laughed; the captain transferred Newton onto another ship. On the other hand, Newton periodically wrote short prayers and devoted himself to Bible study.

Each period of peaceful contemplation was countered by spiritual upheaval … and then the event that changed his life occurred. John Newton's own words best relate the incident on the *Greyhound*, March 24, 1748:

"The ship I was on board as a passenger, was on a trading voyage for gold, ivory, dyers wood, and bees wax. We were off the coast of Newfoundland [Canada]. On these banks we stopped half a day to fish for cod. I went to bed that night in my usual security and indifference, but was awakened from a sound sleep by the force of a violent sea which broke on board us; so much of it came down below as filled the cabin I lay in with water. This alarm was followed by a cry from the deck, that the ship was going down or sinking. The sea had torn away the upper timbers on one side. It was astonishing, and almost miraculous, that any of us survived to relate the story. We had but eleven or twelve people to bale the water with buckets and pails.

"Hours later, being almost spent with cold and labour, I went to speak with the captain, who was busied elsewhere, and just as I was returning from him, I said, almost without any meaning, 'If this will not do, the Lord have mercy upon us.' This was the first desire I had breathed for mercy for the space of many years. I was instantly struck with my own words and thought 'What mercy can there be for me?' I was obliged to return to the pump, and there I continued till noon, almost every passing wave breaking over my head; but we made ourselves fast with ropes, that we might not be washed away. I thought, if the Christian religion was true, I could not be forgiven;

and was, therefore, expecting, and almost at times wishing, to know the worst of it."

Newton continued to bail water and stuff leaks with clothing and bedding until noon the next day. After resting, he steered the ship until midnight. At the helm, he had time for reflection, and he waited in fear for the vessel to sink. By six o'clock in the evening the storm passed and "there arose a gleam of hope."

The battered vessel was still far from England's shores. Wooden casks of provisions had been beaten to pieces by the violent waves, and livestock had been washed overboard. The cod the sailors caught off Newfoundland, and the bit of fresh water left, kept the crew alive.

As the *Greyhound* limped into an Irish port, "our very last victuals were boiling in the pot," wrote Newton, and another storm arose. "If we had continued at sea that night in our enfeebled condition, we must have gone to the bottom.

"About this time I began to know that there is a God that hears and answers prayers." For the rest of his long life, John Newton observed the anniversary of the storm date, for "on that day the Lord sent from on high, and delivered me out of the deep waters."

It was fitting that John Newton, rowdy seaman, found direction for his future onboard a ship named for a breed of dog. In Christian symbolism, the dog is a faithful companion and also represents guidance and priests. Also, dogs, like vultures, were believed to accompany the dead. The fleet-footed greyhound is known for its superior eyesight.

How appropriate, then, that during a horrific storm at sea, John Newton gained the vision that would lead him to the ministry his mother had planned for so long before.

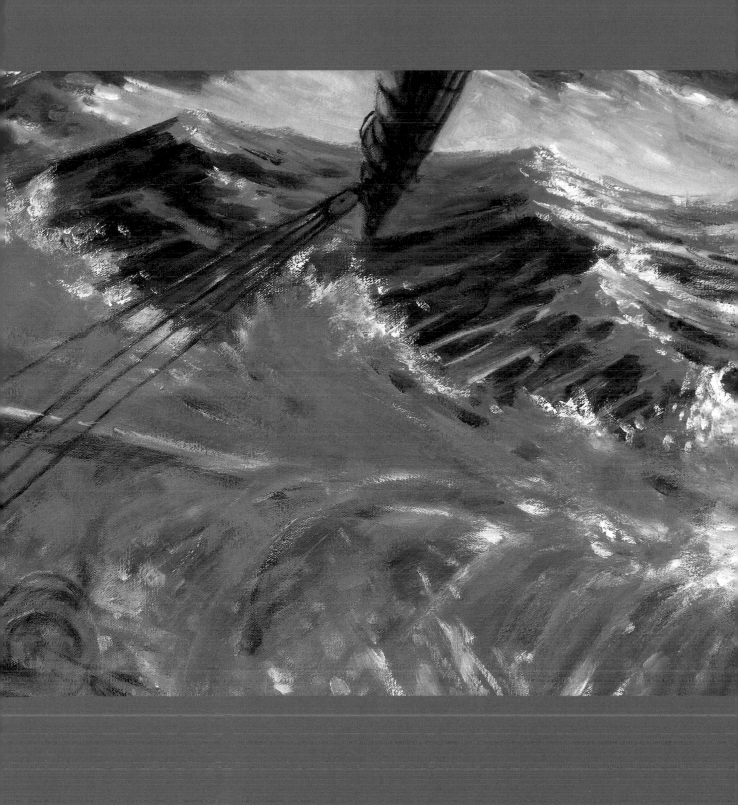

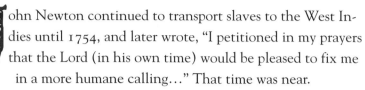

John Newton continued to transport slaves to the West Indies until 1754, and later wrote, "I petitioned in my prayers that the Lord (in his own time) would be pleased to fix me in a more humane calling…" That time was near.

Ready for a fourth voyage to Africa, Newton became ill. He resigned his command the day before the ship sailed: the person who was hired as captain in his place, most of the officers, and many of the crew died "and the vessel was brought home with great difficulty."

Newton never sailed the seas again. He lived with his wife, Mary, in Liverpool, where, for nine years, he was the Tide Surveyor. During this period, Newton felt he was called to the ministry. Like many ordinary English citizens, he was attracted to the new kind of religion preached about in the streets and the fields by George Whitefield and John Wesley, who founded the Methodist church.

Newton was also caught up in the evangelical religions of the time, offshoots of the Church of England that scorned frivolous activities and believed that poverty was good for the soul. The common people, overpowered by the masters of industry, would be rewarded in Heaven for their earthly suffering. Bible-reading and hymn-singing were important aspects of this popular movement.

At the age of thirty-nine, John Newton was ordained and appointed curate of the Parish Church of St. Peter and St. Paul in Olney, England, a town that soon became the home of poet William Cowper. Periodically insane throughout his long life, Cowper described the place as "inhabited chiefly by the half-starved and ragged of the earth," or, in other words, audiences eager to hear how they could be lifted from their wretchedness. Newton and Cowper became friends and lived in houses with adjoining back gardens. Cowper wrote poetry; Newton wrote sermons. Both men enjoyed walks in the fields and woods, where they reflected on Nature and God away from the distractions of daily life.

John Newton's reputation as a powerful speaker drew hundreds of listeners who filled the church to overflowing. In his study, an attic room of the vicarage, Newton wrote new hymns. Above the fireplace, Newton painted two quotes from the Bible, including a reminder of his own enslavement: "But thou shalt remember that thou wast a bond-man in the land of Egypt, and the Lord thy God redeemed thee" (Deut. 15:15).

In 1771, Newton invited Cowper to join him in publishing a book of their hymns. However, Cowper suffered a recurrence of his mental illness and Newton carried on alone. The completed book of nearly 350 hymns was published eight years later as *Olney Hymns*. In his preface, Newton set the record straight: He had seen his hymns printed elsewhere, with other people's names on them. And he clearly marked the hymns written by Cowper with a large "C." The book's simply expressed material, wrote Newton, was for "plain people," and he worried about offending "readers of taste."

Divided into three sections, or books, the hymns were formed around Scripture, seasons, and a variety of subjects about faith. Hymn 41 in Book I was about "Faith's Review and Expectation," and the suggested Scripture passage was 1 Chron. 17:16, 17. Then appeared the words that over two hundred years later continue to bring solace and joy to people of all denominations: "Amazing grace! (How sweet the sound!)"....

Newton's Hymn 41, known to us as "Amazing Grace," was not selected for unique treatment during his lifetime. The *Olney Hymns* were shared among the community during weekly services. John Newton continued to minister to the parish families until 1780, when he was sent to be the rector of the Parish of St. Mary Woolnoth, in London. There, as before, the eloquent Newton attracted crowds, and among the listeners was William Wilberforce.

Young Wilberforce, a newly elected member of Parliament, was already devoting himself to social reform. A friend of John Wesley, Wilberforce was influenced by Newton's sermons and became active in the growing English movement to abolish slavery.

Newton, experienced in all aspects of "the triangular trade," wrote a pamphlet in 1788 entitled "Thoughts Upon the African Slave Trade." He confessed how "disagreeable I had long found the trade; but I think I should have quitted it sooner, had I considered it as I now do, to be unlawful and wrong. But I never had a scruple upon this head at the time ... what I did I did ignorantly."

In "Thoughts," Newton described the coast of the slave trade in sometimes surprising ways. For example, he lamented the fact that too many seamen died as a result of the "African trade," and England was being drained of young men and boys. In fact, not until a few pages into the pamphlet did Newton discuss the treatment of the captives. He argued that he had lived among the Africans and been more secure than among those in a "civilized nation [England]." Newton confessed that the Africans were cheated and that some were kidnapped. He described a slave's horrible life on a slave ship. He admitted that many might have preferred to stay onboard, had they known the toil, hunger, and tortures they would endure as slaves. He condemned his past life.

John Newton presented evidence against the slave trade to parliamentary committees. By 1792, nearly half a million British citizens had signed petitions to end the slave trade. The same year, some of the states in North America banned slave trading. Despite everything, the abolitionists were defeated several times. Even Wilberforce became discouraged.

John Newton was growing old. His sight, hearing, and memory were failing him; however, he continued to preach. Depressions and periods when he failed to recognize friends occurred more often. By 1800, Newton's wife, Mary, and friend Cowper had died. The French Revolution, and Napoleon Bonaparte, had changed Europe.

John Newton died in 1807 at age eighty-two. That same year, Britain abolished the slave trade at home and in all British colonies. William Wilberforce died in 1833, the year the Slavery Abolition Act was passed and slaves in the British Empire were freed. Other countries around the world enacted similar laws.

John Newton summarized his life in his epitaph, which reads in part:

*John Newton, Clerk,*
*Once an infidel and libertine,*
*A servant of slaves in Africa,*
*Was by the rich mercy of our Lord and Saviour*
*Jesus Christ,*
*Preserved, restored, pardoned,*
*And appointed to preach the faith he*
*Had long laboured to destroy...*

For centuries, "Amazing Grace" has been a part of our lives. We sing it at social and religious occasions, at christenings and weddings. We hear it at the funerals of our veterans of past wars and those service members killed, more recently, in Iraq and Afghanistan. There are arrangements for many musical instruments and foreign languages. "Amazing Grace" has traveled through time, from Newton's choir to a twenty-first-century listener's portable media player.

There is absolutely no doubt that John Newton wrote the words of the hymn, for his was a well-documented life. The story of the music we sing to Newton's words, however, is still debated.

During Newton's lifetime, hymnbooks didn't have musical notes or scores. In fact, *Olney Hymns* looks like a book of poetry. People changed the printed verses, imitating the singing of each line by a leader. It's easy to imagine how much noise resulted from all the untrained voices echoing the often on-the-spot compositions of a deacon.

Gradually, hymnals were printed with musical notes. Sometimes, the new words were set to familiar folk tunes.

Singing outside of church became more popular through the eighteenth and nineteenth centuries. New hymns, with original scores, were written. Well-loved hymns were incorporated into family reunions and social sing-along sessions. Music traveled through the generations and beloved songs survived.

There is plenty of speculation about the life of "Amazing Grace." Some say the music developed from songs actually chanted by the African natives on their way to the New World. Some guess it was a ballad tune from another country matched with Newton's words. Others wonder if it was a song sung by the slaves in the southern United States before the Civil War.

The source of the music doesn't really matter. "Amazing Grace" is a hymn that has fulfilled our needs for a long time. Some have thought the word *wretch* is too strong; however, those who turn to the hymn for sustenance, for peace, identify with the word as Newton did. What human hasn't at one point in his or her life felt some kind of despair? Wretchedness is not just a concept from Newton's time. It has been and continues to be a common state in human history. "Amazing Grace" proves the point by becoming increasingly popular during periods of social strife, like during the civil-rights demonstrations of the 1960s.

The earth's inhabitants, whether affiliated with a faith or not, share the desire for guidance, joy, freedom, and peace. Tempest-tossed John Newton, admittedly an imperfect man but ever a hopeful and focused spirit, gave us all those when he wrote "Amazing Grace."

Amazing grace! (How sweet the sound!)
That sav'd a wretch like me!
I once was lost, but now am found;
Was blind, but now I see.
'Twas grace that taught my heart to fear,
And grace my fears reliev'd;

How precious did that grace appear,
The hour I first believ'd!
Through many dangers, toils, and snares,
I have already come;
'Tis grace has brought me safe thus far,
And grace will lead me home.

The Lord has promis'd good to me,
His word my hope secures:
He will my shield and portion be,
As long as life endures.
Yes, when this flesh and heart shall fail,
And mortal life shall cease;

I shall possess, within the veil,
A life of joy and peace.
The earth shall soon dissolve like snow,
The sun forbear to shine:
But God, who call'd me here below,
Will be for ever mine.

race, the divine love and protection bestowed freely by God, was something the young, enslaved John Newton sorely needed as he toiled in the blazing sun. Little did he know that years after he was forced to plant lime trees on a plantation, he would return to Sierra Leone, a free man, to see the mature trees, laden with fruit, reaching towards the heavens. John Newton had survived to gather both the limes and God's mercy. Many of those who had been slaves came to rejoice in a newfound freedom, the result of governments finally recognizing the dignity of each human life.

A sad but true coda to John Newton's story is that today, around the world, millions of people are still illegally enslaved by those more powerful than they. The weak, the young, the poor, and the uneducated are still kidnapped or sold into slavery. The cries of pain and fear heard long ago from the slave ships echo still.

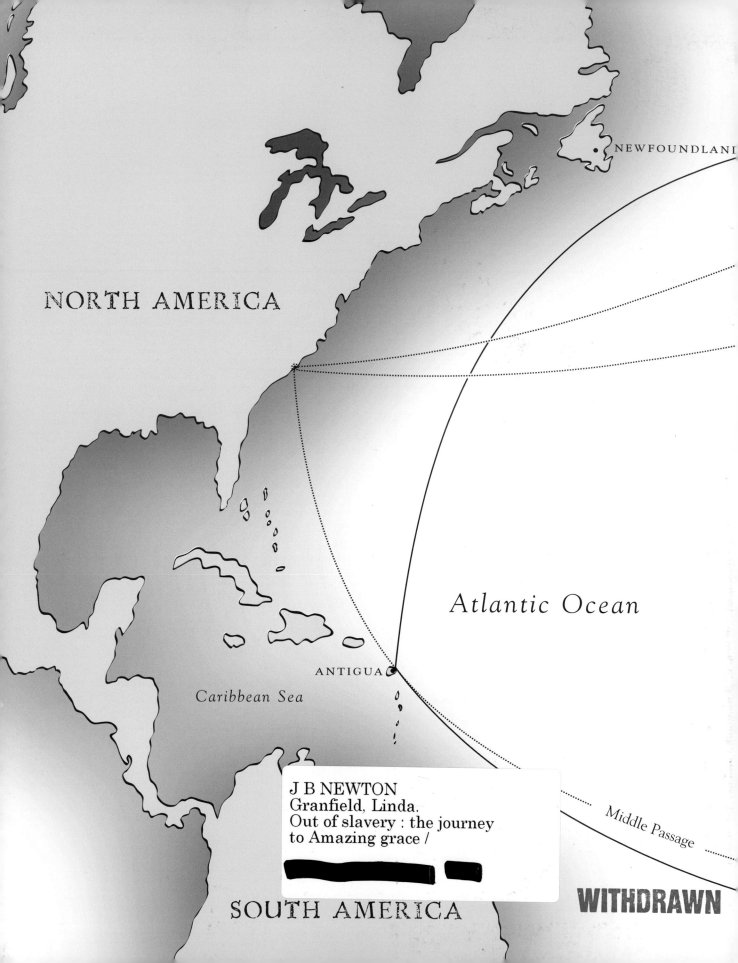

NEWFOUNDLAND

NORTH AMERICA

Atlantic Ocean

ANTIGUA

Caribbean Sea

Middle Passage

SOUTH AMERICA